Swans and Storks
Sparrows and Doves

Karl König

Swans and Storks
Sparrows and Doves
Sketches for an Imaginative Zoology

Floris Books

First published in German as essays
in *Die Drei* between 1956 and 1966.
First published in volume form as *Bruder Tier*
by Verlag Freies Geistesleben, Stuttgart, 1967.

This volume, consisting of three of the eleven essays
in *Bruder Tier*, first published in English in 1987.

'Swans and Storks' and 'The Sparrows of the Earth'
were translated by Richard Aylward.
'The Dove as a Sacred Bird' was first published in
the *Golden Blade* 1968.

British Library CIP Data

König, Karl
Swans and storks, sparrows and doves:
sketches for an imaginative zoology.
1. Birds
I. Title
598   QL673

ISBN 0–86315–046–2

Printed in Great Britain
by Billing & Sons Ltd, Worcester

Contents

References

The system used in the book quotes author and year of publication, followed by volume (if necessary) and page. The full title and publication details are in the bibliography. References to lectures by Rudolf Steiner include the date of the lecture in square brackets.

Foreword

In 1928 Karl König came to London to take part in a conference together with other followers of the spiritual teacher Rudolf Steiner. It was typical of this twenty-six-year-old Viennese doctor that he should make time on his first visit to have a look round the squalid East End of the city. He poured out his heart to Friedrich Rittelmeyer, father figure and founder of The Christian Community, about the misery and suffering he felt crying out for help in the slums. But König not only had a capacity for compassion but a flair for dynamic leadership, enabling him to put into practice his ideals for forming a community life that would include the deprived. When, ten years later, an empty manse on an estate in Scotland was made available to him it became the first base for his work with children and others needing the special care and attention of a devoted community to live in. This work developed by leaps and bounds until the Camphill community has become recognized throughout the world for its valuable contribution in founding villages and schools where its principles can be lived.

As a lecturer and occasional writer, Karl König was inspired by Anthroposophy, taught by Rudolf Steiner, but he also has a unique spiritual 'eye' of his own. He was filled with brotherly kinship not only towards the human being in need, but also towards the animals. During the last ten years of his life, he worked intermittently on a series of what eventually became eleven essays about animals. These were put together after his death in 1966 under the title *Bruder Tier* (Brother Animal). For

9

this first English edition, to be published in three separate volumes, only very small revisions have been made. Despite the passing of time, we have here real treasure. Nothing quite comparable on animals is to be found anywhere else. The often unique insights of Anthroposophy, the mythological archetypes, the scientific wonders are all infused with much compassion and understanding for the true being of animals. Karl König seems to get right inside their skins (scales, fur or feathers) and experiences from there new horizons of consciousness. I feel sure he would still love them as his brothers even if they had not been, as he so deftly portrayed, of such vital importance for human life and the continued evolution of the earth.

Michael Jones

Swans and Storks

1 The world of the birds

Even as children we noticed that spring was coming when the birds began to arrive from the south. Outside the sun rose ever higher, and deep in the soul joy arose. The birds as they returned brought back the growing light to us children. Spring and the awakening of the bird world belonged together. The fact that other animals reappeared was — apart from the butterflies, which heralded summer — not so important.

For a long time the return of the birds and of the sun must have been bound together for the human soul: it was as though the intensifying light and warmth embraced the bird world within them. Just as the fishes belong to the water, so do the birds belong to the life of the air, pervaded by light and warmth. That is their kingdom. Here too, as everywhere in the realm of creation, there are exceptions, but they serve only to prove the rule.

In this realm of air, light, and warmth the birds develop the special activity — flying — for which they are well equipped. Usually a bird does not have to learn to fly; it flies naturally. A chick is at first unable to get itself into the air, not because it cannot fly but because its body is too heavy for its undeveloped wings. A growing bird never has to learn flying from its parents, unlike the young seal, who is coaxed for weeks by the mother to get into the water and attempt to swim.

A bird flies, as fish swim; its feathers carry it through the air. It has only to give itself up to them to progress forwards. It is this submission to the feathers which makes flying a matter of course for the bird. The plumage is spread across its body like a wonderful garment which carries it over lands and seas, as flying carpets do in fairy tales. What the bird has to do is to make itself part of the warmth and the air currents which flow across the earth so that they carry it along. It experiences the wind as it blows, the weaving of the warmth, the shimmering of the heat: its being is united with them.

The muscles of a bird's breast and limbs are astonishingly delicate in contrast to the power they would have to produce if it were only muscle-power which enables a bird to fly. The wings are needed for take-off and landing; flying is achieved by the feathers. They are a mysterious structure, formed only after completion of the main phases of the development of the embryo. They are added to the bird's body as it were from the outside, giving it form and structure, and gradually clothing the naked miserable body in beauty and dignity. The plumage is like a coat woven from powers which do not belong to earth and water, but to air, warmth, and light.

Thus we can understand Rudolf Steiner's saying (1970, 89f [1923 Oct 27]) that the bird experiences its bones and organs somewhat as we experience burdens such as suitcases or rucksacks we have to carry. 'You would not call this luggage your body. In the same way the bird, in speaking of itself, would only speak of the warmth-imbued air, and of everything else as the luggage which it bears about with it in earthly existence.'

The bird identifies itself solely with the air which it breathes in and warms through. Everything else is foreign to it, not its own, but its burden. But this 'luggage', the bird's body, is constructed in a special way.

A bird's organs are all packed together in a small space; one might almost say that they are stowed in the 'rucksack' between the breast and the abdomen. Here are the heart and stomach, lungs and intestines, kidneys and reproductive organs. This space is almost completely enclosed by the ribs and sealed off at the front by a powerful breastbone. There is no bladder, so that urine and excrement are passed through a single channel. Neither is there a colon, and the breast is not separated from the abdomen by a diaphragm.

By contrast, the head is extended on a neck which may often look too long, or is sometimes quite short. The head is not really a head in the strict sense, but more like an appendage, a stem with eyes in it, hardening into a beak towards the front. This beak determines to a large extent the physiognomy of the particular genus and species. One recognizes a bird by its plumage but only the beak indicates its parentage.

The limbs, when featherless, appear wretched and stunted. Since the legs remain unfledged for the most part, they are often disappointingly gaunt. To the observer they seem poor, old, and helpless.

The arms with the feathers removed can only be compared to malformations. When fledged they exemplify the power, beauty, and grace of the bird. Displayed in these wings is the true nature of the bird genus. They carry it through the air; they give it life in the element of warmth and light.

For this reason Gerlach is right when, in the introduction to his fine bird book (1953), he writes: 'The birds are of lighter stuff than ours. They do not walk on heavy soles over the earth. Most of them touch the ground lightly with their toes, always ready to swing aloft. The air for them is space for unbounded movement, wherever they wish to go.'

This 'lighter' material is in fact a mineralized substance; for example, a bird passes excrement almost wholly encrusted with uric salts. Everything about the body is as if dehydrated. The skin has no sweat glands; the feathers are a mineralized callosity; the legs and toes are bony and sclerotic.

The body is filled with air, even the shafts of the tubular bones, by means of a system of air-sacs. Thus, the bird's body becomes a balloon which can easily raise itself into the air and float there. For this reason the breath and the organs connected with it are the centre of a bird's life.

This body-build gives rise to the second activity — song — for which the bird genus is uniquely competent. No other creature comes near it on this score. Some species, such as parrots and budgerigars, ravens and starlings, can do more than sing: they imitate the sounds of the human voice so well that they achieve something like pronunciation. This has nothing to do with real speech: it springs from the bird's capacity for relating itself intimately to the realm of sound. It can do this because sound is carried by the air, as is the bird itself. Sound and air, song and flight, are expressive of the airy world in which wind and warmth and light are in constant interplay.

In this element the birds have their existence. They surround the earth with their flight and song. To imagine the atmosphere without birds is an abstraction. The songs and cries, whistles and calls, croaking and screeching of the birds belong to the air, as do their flying and wing-beats, fluttering, hovering, and flitting. Thus the bird genus fills the air-space of our planet.

2 Feeding and nesting habits

The bird touches the earth at only one point. Not where its toes just touch it; that is a very fleeting and superficial contact. Hopping and tripping and putting one leg in front of the other are not contact. These movements arise from the necessary search for food; not the bird but the beak itself makes these actions necessary. The nest, by contrast, is a structure which makes the bird an earth-dwelling creature. Nests are built from every conceivable kind of substance — soil and mud, twigs and small stones, moss and leaves, dung and sand. The form and type of nest is as varied as the species and genus of birds; each genus builds its own type of nest.

To this nest is entrusted the clutch (a number of eggs which is characteristic for each species) and then the time of brooding begins. Within the confines of the nest a cloak of warmth is created — a kind of oven in which the coming generations are sufficiently baked. It is an archetypal baking process that goes on here. What the elements themselves see to in the case of fish and newts, reptiles and all invertebrates, is here carried out by the individual bird. The mammal has transferred this process into the female organism, where the womb has become an organic nest. The bird builds itself a structure which it turns into an incubator for a few weeks of the year. It then becomes the medium through which the bird makes contact with the earthly realm. Here the otherwise homeless becomes, for a while, settled and earthbound.

Two sorts of young emerge from the eggs. One group is unfledged and helpless. The other, covered with fluff and down, is perky and immediately ready for life and action. We refer to the first group as heterophagous (needing to be fed by others) and to the second group as autophagous (able to feed itself). Lorenz Oken divided birds into these two great categories. But his ideas on this subject, developed at length in his massive work on natural history (1837), are not always correct; between the heterophagous and the autophagous young there are many transitions, and his system of classification, attempted more than a hundred years ago, is no longer valid (see Makatsch 1954). In this duality, nevertheless, there is hidden a valuable principle: we must only learn to understand it in the right way. The duality exists among many species right through all classes of animals, in the context of the first encounter of the new-born with the world.

Thus, for example, we have the embryo of the kangaroo, so dependent that it creeps into its mother's pouch and holds fast with its lips to her breast; or the beasts of prey, born blind and helpless, in contrast to the hoofed animals which are agile and quickly get on to their feet. A hetrerophagous creature is often a kind of larva which needs protection in order gradually to reach its final form.

In birds this process occurs through the development of plumage, which grows out over the small pitiable body, enveloping it by degrees until the bird is ready to fly. The feathers are of two types — soft down and stiff contour-feathers. The down feathers, more like a fluff which covers and warms, come first. The contour-feathers grow very gradually and form the actual flight-feathers. The well-known ostrich feathers consist of down and so are of no use for flying.

What then is it that separates autophagous from the heterophagous birds? Not simply the capacity, or the lack of it, to live without protection when they are born. It is something else, which points to the growth process of the individual species and is deeply involved with it.

The autophagous birds are much more closely connected to the earth than are the heterophagous. Autophagous birds do not need to wait until their plumage is complete before they can move. They slip out of the egg and at once begin their activities. The little chick pecks and hops about; it cheeps tirelessly, and although it follows the mother, it has already become independent. So it is that ducklings go into the pond and cygnets are so far advanced on the first day that they can be taken by the parents on to the water. Flying, if it develops at all, comes later and is then acquired. It is not absolutely necessary as the expression of the bird's motor activity.

The heterophagous birds, on the other hand, are strangers to the earth. They are born into the nest as bundles of flesh. They would lie there helpless if the parents did not help to keep growth going. Their food has to be

16

predigested and placed in their open beaks. The accumulating dung has to be removed by the mother with her beak and put out of the nest. On cool days the incubator is started up again and surrounds the young with warmth, since they are not yet capable of producing their own warmth. Only when the plumage, flight feathers and tail feathers are all full-grown is the heterophagous bird a complete bird, capable at last of living in its own element of light, air and warmth.

Hence we could speak of autophagous birds as being more suited to earthly life and more integrated into the earthly element. The heterophagous birds, by contrast, have remained more cosmic; they withdraw from the earth and want to connect themselves with it only when their plumage has fully developed.

The plumage is like a mantle drawn over a bird after it has slipped out of the egg. The feathers come as from outside, from the surroundings. For this reason Rudolf Steiner says clearly (1963, 157 [1911 Aug 26]):

> The plumage is formed from without, and a feather can only come into being because the forces which work down upon the Earth from cosmic space are stronger than the forces coming from the Earth.
> The framework of the feather, what one may call its quill or spine, is of course subject to certain forces coming from the Earth, but it is the cosmic forces which contribute what is attached to the quill and constitute the bird's plumage.

These cosmic formative forces, which equip the growing bird with its coat of feathers, come from those regions from which the bird-beings have never quite separated themselves. For it cannot have happened that the birds in the past raised themselves from the earth into the air, that is developing from primitive reptile forms in such a way that in the course of countless years wings grew on them and then they learnt to fly. Such a picture is not merely unbiological; it is also — correctly viewed

— quite untenable. The birds developed out of the air downwards towards the earth. They originated in the heights and have related themselves to a greater or lesser degree with the earth. An archaeopteryx was never an archetypal bird, but rather a bird-form which fell too far and thereby took on reptilian characteristics. It was the end of a developmental process, not the beginning. The archaeopteryx has died out because it could not live on. Unlike man and the mammals, the birds have never really taken to and accepted the earth.

Rudolf Steiner wished to indicate this when he said (1982, 145 [1909 July 1]): 'But in the bird nature we have beings that did not assume the lowest functions; instead they overshot the mark in the opposite direction. They failed to descend far enough, as it were . . . But as evolution continued, outer conditions compelled them to solidify . . .'

Only now does the fundamental principle of the bird world become evident. They are creatures which have approached earthly existence but have never been able to make it their own. They are beings which have been involved in the process of becoming animal, but have not carried this to its earthly conclusion. Had they done so, they would have thrown off their coat of feathers, as do the seven ravens and the six swans in the fairy-tale. So the birds keep their plumage, as do the mammals their hair and the reptiles and fish their scales. They remain in their enchantment, some raised too high, others sunk too low.

The autophagous birds were on their way to earth; they sought it without ever reaching it. The heterophagous birds, by contrast, were afraid of too strong a union with the watery and earthy elements. So they have to lie helpless in an earthly nest, until their plumage comes to their aid, raises them, and gives them wings.

3 The swan

The great family of the swans, which inhabits many parts of the world, belongs to the extensive order of geese and ducks. We know some of the many species of this group; they range from the Arctic over the northern regions of Asia, Europe and America, and across the Equator into the southern continents. Only around the South Pole are they absent. The eider-ducks, the divers, and the mallards we know, and the domestic goose, to mention only a few names. They indicate something of the rich variety of species, colouring, and life-styles to be found in this order.

We are familiar with the activities of wild ducks on the ponds and lakes of the plains and in the mountains. They live also in the bays and among the dunes by the sea, and in autumn they fly in thousands on their journey south.

Their natural home is that boundary region between air and water where the air borders the reflecting surface of lakes, ponds, rivers and seas. All birds of the goose family can swim; almost all can fly, although flying is often harder for them than swimming. Especially taking to the air and landing are slow and laborious; the wings have to make enormous efforts, and the feet — sliding over the water — have to assist until a certain height is reached. Then progress is easy; with necks stretched out forwards and feet tucked in, the flight of ducks goes swiftly by.

A duck's beak is as long as its head, broadening out slightly to the front, and is covered with a sensitive soft skin. The feet are short, often set far back, so that walking is akin to waddling. The four toes are webbed and give the feet a clumsy appearance. Walking is not the business of ducks; they are all swimmers and divers; their life is played out on the water. Only for the purpose of building nests and brooding do they go ashore; some even retire deep into the shelter of neighbouring woods or marshes

19

or into hollow trees. The young are autophagous. A few hours after hatching they are ready to go into the water with the parents and they know exactly how to paddle and dive.

Swans are one part of this order. They are akin to ducks and geese, and yet different from them. They give an immediate impression of exclusiveness carried to the point of ostentation. One can understand that in Great Britain swans are the property of the Crown. They are royal visitors, envoys of a higher power. They have something unapproachable which surrounds them, as they glide over the water in their proud beauty. Then a swan's body, clothed in white or dark feathers, is like a boat which glides along, while head and beak are carried like a figurehead on the long, curved neck — a proud, often powerful sight, especially when the wings, slightly raised and extended like a shield, shelter the moving body.

The swans belong to the largest birds of their order. They are mostly monogamous; a mated pair may stay together for years. If migration occurs in the autumn (this happens only in the northerly regions of the earth), the swans will return together to the old nest, to keep the eggs warm for six to eight weeks, and to raise the young. Once the young swans have become somewhat independent, they are left by the parents and are treated as strangers. To become aware of their nobility, they must from now on master being alone.

Brehm (1911) describes the distribution of swans in the following way:

> The swans of the nine species described inhabit all parts of the earth except the tropics, especially the cold and temperate zones of the northern hemisphere. The area of distribution for each species is very extensive and the regular journeys of the swans cover long distances. All species migrate, but not under all circumstances. It is not uncommon for some to stay in the same country through the

winter, or at least they roam only within a small territory.

We know above all the humped swan, which lives on our ponds and in our estuaries. Large groups often take over a wide expanse of water. They seek the vicinity of human settlements. Small rivers which flow past old town walls, fish-ponds near monasteries, quiet ponds in old gardens, remote estuaries on which old villages nestle — these are their home. The snow-white plumage, the red beak, and the dark hump on the beak give this swan his aristocratic bearing.

Further to the north live the somewhat smaller whistling swans (*Cygnus musicus*). They belong to the species of which the Greeks used to say that they came with Apollo to Delphi every year from the north; the god was swept along on their wings, bringing tidings from the land of the Hyperboreans. Many observers tell of the strange, sometimes bell-like voice of this species; and it is said of them that they sing when their comrades are about to die. During the winter they leave their home in Iceland and Scandinavia for the regions of Central Europe. They are at home as far away as Russia and Siberia.

The black-necked swan nests in South America, from Peru to the Falkland Islands, and in Brazil. Its plumage is white, but the neck and head are covered with black feathers. The hump on the greyish-yellow beak is red, and the wings are short, yet it is a good flyer.

The dark-coloured mourning-swan lives in South Australia and Tasmania. Underneath a covering of blackish-brown feathers the white flight-feathers stand out, and speak of its brothers living in the north.

This picture of their geographical distribution shows clearly that swans belong to the north. The whistling swan lives right up in the Arctic region. The temperate zones are the habitat of the humped swans. The tropics are uninhabited by swans. Further south, we find the two dark-coloured species which belong in South America and Australia: the black-necked and the mourning swans. This distribution gives an impressive picture of swans all round the earth.

Although swans are water-birds, they need the land for nesting and breeding. But they never take off from land; they use the water as their runway, and they always land on water, though they have been seen to take to the air and to land on ice.

It is understandable that these noble birds have been held sacred. The beauty and dignity which they radiate call forth in men a feeling which points to something higher. The swan is by no means a gentle lord. He is quick to attack, strong and easily aroused to anger. He then lets fly in a rage with wings and beak, and even takes on more powerful opponents. His white plumage gives him an aura of invincibility; his courage makes him a knight.

Do we not feel, when we look at the swan, that there are higher regions of soul than the everyday? In ordinary life, we are geese and ducks, stupid and unconcerned, joyful or painfully moved. But beyond all this lives the swan in us. The exalted bird of the soul which comes from the far north and often visits us only as a guest before going on further. In the Middle Ages, if we wished to dedicate ourselves to this idea of the swan, we would have become a member of one of the many orders of Swan Knights which existed then. The bird on their coat of arms was the white swan, which enjoined the knights to raise themselves above the goose and duck existence, and to lead their lives in proud service.

4 The stork

A quite different air plays round the stork. What a difference between the swan gliding silently along and the stork stepping across marshy meadows! The swan hides its short clumsy legs, which are useful only for paddling. The stork walks as if on stilts, which are painted red to make them stand out. The stork's beak is as long as its legs, and often so big and heavy (for example in the marabou) that it tilts the bird's head downwards.

A general feature of the build of birds is indicated here: the shape and size of the beak and of the legs correspond to each other. If the beak is small, the feet and legs are also small. The hard curved beak of the birds of prey is reflected in the claws. This harmony between two distinctive features of birds is especially evident in the stork.

It is a strange order to which the storks belong. They are referred to as Ciconiiformes or Gressores, a name which points to their special feature — their gait. Four families make up this order: herons, ibis, hammerheads, and storks. These birds are all essentially of one type, with relatively long, thin legs, and long, pointed beaks. Neck, head, and beak are almost like a limb which seizes food with fast serpentine movements. The Gressores are birds of prey. They eat everything which moves around them: frogs and small toads, worms, lizards, beetles, mussels, fish, even young birds, young hares, moles and mice. A blow or a stab with the beak and the prey is quickly consumed. This behaviour belies their appearance; storks look tamer than they really are. But the red colouring which occurs in various parts of the body in some species gives a hint of their aggressive, warlike nature. One could classify them as cruel melancholics. Shallow ponds, lakes or rivers are their hunting-ground. They live on the shores or river banks among reeds and rushes, papyrus and willows.

These birds, with few exceptions, build their nests high in the tops of trees or on roofs, as does the stork which has become a close neighbour of man. Large branches and twigs are collected for the nest, which is usually round, and lined with moss and dung, straw and leaves.

The young are heterophagous. During the first weeks they lie there helplessly; they have to be fed and cleaned by the parents and also need the parents' protection against excessive cold or heat. We owe to Horst Siewert (1955) such detailed observations of black and white storks that we are familiar with this process in every detail. He describes how frogs, which have been predigested in the stomach of the parents, are regurgitated, cut into small pieces and pushed into the open beaks of the hungry young. We are told also how on cool evenings, the parents sit on the nest so as to warm the young; on hot days, when the sun shines on the eyrie, they perch on the edge of the nest in such a way that the nestlings lie in their shadow.

It takes several weeks for the contour-feathers to grow and for the legs to be strong enough to take the first steps on the edge of the nest. The young black stork, with its clumsy wings, then flies quickly from one branch to the next in the tree where the nest is, and returns to the nest. Until one day, suddenly, parents and children set off together to hunt for prey.

The Gressores, including the heron and the ibis, are at home all over the world, except for the far north. Their habitat is always a region between shallow water and land. Where marshes and fens are formed and the earth element and the water element meet, there tread the feet of the Gressores, and their beaks penetrate into this area of organic life. They have, as it were, descended one level lower than the ducks, for ducks come down only as far as the boundary between air and water.

However, it is only with foot and beak that the Gressores penetrate where earth and water meet; otherwise they remain connected always with the air. Then for building their nest they rise to the tops of the trees, there to wait and care for their young.

The storks are the only birds in this order which at least attempt to draw near to the earth by coming close to man, as the white stork does. They build their nests on the roofs of houses and stables and return year after year to the old nest. Children love them and expect them to bring them brothers and sisters. And the grown-ups smile at this superstition or condemn this nonsense.

Can we ascribe to this presumption of the intellect the fact that the stork is gradually ceasing to frequent the dwellings of Central and Northern Europe and withdraws ever more from them? We know very well that the stork does not bring our children, but what was it that gave rise to this inner picture for such a long time? Siewert (1955) describes an experience which might perhaps put us on the track of an answer:

> In a small Pomeranian town the storks appeared just as school had finished. The children poured out on to the streets, and a little lad who soon spotted the large birds cried out his discovery to the world. All eyes were raised, and all the children laughed at the sight of the long-legged birds in the clear bright sky. But it was not only the children who were glad; many people gazed up from the narrow streets and forgot that only the day before yesterday the last snow had fallen and that the air was still bitterly cold. Even if the people did not sink to their knees at the first sight of the storks, as they had done two thousand years ago in honour of the bearers of the spring, at least the joy has remained to this present day, for, just as in ancient times, the wanderers brought the spring to this northerly land, with the sun and warmth of the south, and the long winter with its terrors was forgotten.

When Siewert says that the storks were the bearers of spring he is quite right, but two or three thousand years ago people fell to their knees at the sight of the birds because they knew that with them the souls of unborn children were approaching the earth, and that the time of pairing was beginning. Out of his spiritual insight Rudolf Steiner indicated that up to the first pre-Christian millennium births among the Germanic tribes were so arranged that they mostly occurred around the time of Christmas.

This mythical truth was spurned and spoiled by the intellect during the last century, until it gave rise to the stupid and indeed ridiculous pictures of the stork carrying the new-born baby in its beak. But behind this we can discern the true announcement which the stork as messenger of the spring once brought to the people of the north. His clattering sound is heard at the time of weddings, and when on Good Friday children parade through village streets with rattles, they remind us of times past.

The white stork was — and sometimes still is — accompanied by his darker brother. The black stork, however, keeps away from people. It builds its nest in certain tall trees in the depths of forests. In the autumn it returns, like its white brother, to Africa. The migrations of the storks have now been well researched. Avoiding the Mediterranean, they pass from north to south on two main flyways. The eastern route leads across Bessarabia, along the Black Sea to Asia Minor, then over Syria and northern Arabia, across the Red Sea to the Sudan, and from there through East Africa to various parts of southern Africa. The western route passes over southern France and Spain to Morocco and Algiers and across the Sahara mainly to Senegal and the Niger.

No other storks go on this long journey, which covers half the globe. Those living in the Sudan and on the Blue and the White Nile do not migrate. Storks such as the marabou also remain where they are and roam around only at specific times of the year. The storks of this family, with unfledged throat and gigantic craw, feed primarily on carrion. Like the vultures (which also have unfledged throats) they seek for game which has been killed and left by other carnivores. All the storks which live in Africa and India have strange forms. Compared to them, the white stork is like a child which has not yet been stricken

26

by the darkness and need of the earth, but has kept its original purity. It is nearer to the archetypal form of the group-being of the storks. The other storks have become too entangled in the muddy realms of the earth. The marabou storks seem to have sunk the lowest. That is why they eat carrion and could be called the hyenas among storks.

The more domesticated stork stands apart. It leaves the regions of Africa, which are well provided with food, and journeys every year to the north, to bring its message to the people.

Since men have started to tread the path towards freedom, however, and their children are born at all times of the year, the mission of the stork has come to an end. Since the beginning of the century they have been disappearing from Central and Northern Europe. They have now begun to settle in southern Africa, and many individual families of storks have been found nesting there. Will they make this land their habitat for ever and forget Europe? The destiny of the group-souls of animals and birds is as diverse as that of individual men. Only sometimes is it granted to us to get a glimpse of their real task.

5 The message of the swans and storks

Among the fairy tales collected by the brothers Grimm is the tale of the six swans. It tells of a king who lost his way while hunting deep in the forest and came to a cottage where a beautiful girl was waiting for him. But her mother was a witch, who forced the king to take her daughter as his bride; only then would he be shown the way out of the dark forest. And so it happened; the king took the beautiful daughter of the witch as his wife, but hid the children from his first marriage — six boys and one girl — in a lonely castle. He was shown the way to the castle by a magic thread, with the help of which he was often able to visit his children. By treachery the wicked woman gained power over the magic thread and enchanted the six boys, who encountered her on the road to the castle, turning them into six swans. The girl, who had stayed at home, was saved from this transformation.

That is the first part of the tale, itself formed from two stories interwoven with each other. The first tale tells of the king, of the man who becomes ensnared in the earthly world of the dark forest and is forced to unite himself with the beautiful appearance, the daughter of original sin. The holy offspring from the first marriage, which was free from sin, are kept in an inaccessible castle. Is not this castle, to be reached only by means of a magic thread, the far north, the mythical land of the Hyperboreans? Magic can indeed enter there and transform the children into swans, but it cannot destroy them. The six enchanted brothers are hidden powers of the soul which are to be redeemed one day. On these powers of the soul — the swans — Apollo travels every year from the North to Delphi, to bring powers of the sun and of renewal to men.

They are the same powers which were acquired by initiates of the third degree, who were called Swans for this reason. Rudolf Steiner (1905 Dec 3) says:

> The third stage of initiation is that of the swan. A 'swan' is he who has progressed so far that all things speak to him, even those which have their consciousness on higher levels . . . One must rise to higher worlds to find the 'I', the names of the other beings. These things speak their own names . . . The swan initiates were no longer allowed to bear their own names, but the whole world revealed its names to them.

This helps us to understand the second story in the fairy tale. The sister of the six swans is given the task of remaining silent for six years — a year of silence for each brother. At the same time she has to sew six shirts from star-shaped flowers. The girl decides to perform these tasks. She goes into the forest, finds herself a seat in a high tree and begins the work. A second king comes with his hunters into the forest; they find the girl and, although she resists, she is fetched down from the tree; the king takes her up on to his horse and makes her his wife. The girl maintains her silence, although the king's wicked mother constantly abuses her and takes away her newly born children. She remains true and loyal to her swans. At last, as she is standing at the stake to be burned, the six years are over. The six swans fly down; the six shirts are thrown to them, and the six brothers are once again united with their sister. Now she is able to speak and to convince her spouse of her innocence. At this, the destiny of the swans is fulfilled.

The obligation to remain silent is found also in the Lohengrin saga. The saga tells of the son of Parsifal who is led by a swan into the land of Brabant in order to establish peace there. He is under a rule of silence, though he has to be silent only about his name.

The tale of the six swans, then, tells two stories. One deals with the enchantment and the other with the redemption of six brothers. The enchantment occurs through the wife of the first king; the redemption through the spouse of the second king, the sister of the six swans. The first part of the tale is a story of pre-Christian man; there the saga of Apollo appears in disguise. The second part reaches into the Christian era and tells the Lohengrin saga in the form of a fairy story. In both parts the swan is mysteriously involved.

There is an indication by Rudolf Steiner in which the deeper background of the medieval swan-knight orders is explained. Here we are told how, during the first few Christian centuries, the barrier between the living and the dead was not so impenetrable as it later became (1947, 13f [1922 July 23]):

The dead remained among the living. Outstanding, revered personalities, during the first period after their death . . . were undergoing, as it were, their novitiate in sainthood.

For the people of that time it was not at all strange to speak of the living dead as of real persons. A certain number of the living dead, especially elect ones, having been born for the spiritual world — were appointed as 'Guardians of the Holy Graal.'

Then it is explained that some men here on Earth became representatives of these guardians, and they were united in the various Orders of the Swan. 'They were persons who wanted the Knights of the Grail to be able to work through them in the physical world.'

That is how a picture of the swan presents itself in connection with the work of the illustrious dead. Its being refers to something departed, something lost to man on earth. The soul feels that it has become a duck or goose in the earthly body; that the swanlike has eluded it, and that the seeking and recovery of this has become its task. The soul identifies itself with the sister of the six swans and can find in her example the power to survive in the pain and poverty of the earth until the lost swan brothers appear to her. So it was that Lohengrin turned to Elsa of Brabant and served in the forces of the Emperor Heinrich I in the battle against the Hungarians. Since then many a swan knight has appeared in times of need and affliction as a messenger of deliverance. The soul can then sew further the shirt of 'star-flowers', so as to be ready for the heavenly wedding at the end of the time of probation.

In pre-Christian times the existing powers of the soul were enchanted. They became the six swans, which in terms of the old initiation could become disenchanted only at the third stage. In Christian times, however, some men succeeded in becoming the bearers or vessels of the exalted dead, and this sometimes without inner schooling.

By this means they became messengers, Knights of the Order of the Swan.

In the medieval Lohengrin epic there is a passage which brings out clearly this Christian power of the swan. As the swan is drawing his lord over the sea in a boat, Lohengrin asks him for food. The swan dips his head beneath the waves:

> As if he perceived fish.
> Look there how a small shoal
> Is borne by the swell into his mouth.
> The knight saw them as dry and clean,
> The swan passes them to the hero with his beak.
> He takes them with eager joy,
> And eats one half and gives the swan the other.
> Never were bird or lord so well fed.

After this repast, the swan begins to sing and now Lohengrin can recognize: 'This is in truth an angel pure, who floats with me upon these waves.'

The stork presents us with a different picture. Its venerable brother, the ibis, was sacred for the ancient Egyptians. They respected it so much that they would embalm the bodies of fallen ibises and lay them in special graves. The death penalty applied to the killing of an ibis, even if this was unintentional. The thrice-great Thoth, whom the Greeks called Hermes Trismegistos, was often represented with the head of an ibis. Even his hieroglyph was a stylized ibis. On his head the Thoth-ibis wore the crescent of the moon, in which the disc of the sun was poised. Thoth was the initiator of Egyptian culture. He was the god of speech and writing and is often represented with a stylus in his hand.

What the ibis was for the Egyptians, the stork became for the peoples of the north. He was wise enough to indicate to them the coming of unborn souls, who were ready to be incarnated on Earth. Although, like the swan, he wore a white garment, he evoked a quite different image for the soul. His were not powers of the heart but powers of wisdom. To the soul he appeared not perpetually young, like the swan, but old and clever like a midwife.

The swan is connected with that which is gone, the stork with the unborn, with that which has not yet come. Ibis and Thoth were related to the moon; the swan to the realm of the sun. So it was that Apollo's swans came out of the realm of the Hyperboreans in the North.

The storks came every year from the southern moon-regions of the Lemurian zone up to the North of Europe. Wisdom and humility were balanced in these migrations. The ascending souls of the dead, while on the way to the realm of the sun, were in the region permeated by the spirit of the swans. The souls returning to earth from the sphere of the moon were related to the storks.

The swan's capacity for sacrifice allowed it to affirm its relation to the earth; it became an autophagous bird. The cleverness of the storks kept them back from too strong a connection with the earth. They remained heterophagous.

That is how these two species come before us, both in their contrast and in their joint effect on the soul. They are like memory-pictures which have remained alive from a past period of human history. Once they were united with the souls of men. But the earth-substances became hard and impenetrable, and only a few human souls could take up and fill out their bodies. Then came the birds: hard horn grew into their etheric wings, which became earthly organs and made it possible for them to encircle the planet. Nevertheless, they remained united with the sun, and thereby with the soul-realm of man.

From then on their destiny took manifold shapes and brought them many tasks. Many were lost; others became songsters; many attached themselves to men, as did the chickens, the doves and pigeons. The storks and swans remained connected to the higher part of the human soul. They indicate human destiny: to be born and die, to be wise but to bear humility in the heart, and one day to become — perhaps — a swan knight. Then the stork will be redeemed.

The Dove as a Sacred Bird

1 The dove in the Bible and in history

Wherever in human settlements there is an open space,
in squares and streets, in yards and gardens, we find
pigeons. They coo and fly, hover and patter before San
Marco in Venice just as they do round Nelson's Column
in Trafalgar Square, in the Tuileries in Paris, or in the
Rathausplatz in Vienna. Many a worthy farmhouse had
its dovecot, and we find the same at the centre of many
a little town or village, not only in Europe, but in Asia,
Africa, and America as well — wherever human beings
gather in permanent settlements. There are many kinds
of domestic pigeon, and they appear to have been the
companions of men for many thousands of years. Their
existence is deeply rooted in the conceptions of myth-
ology, and can be followed far back into the first begin-
nings of human history.

In the Old Testament the dove appears in connection
with the end of the Flood. Noah, when the first mountain
tops had appeared above the sinking waters, and the
raven had flown to and fro, released a dove. But she
returned, for she 'found no place to set her foot'. Seven
days later, when another dove had been sent, she 'came
back to him in the evening, and lo, in her mouth a freshly
plucked olive leaf'. But Noah still waited, and after seven
days let another dove fly out, which did not return to the
ark; 'and Noah removed the covering of the ark, and
looked, and behold, the face of the ground was dry.'
(Gen. 8:9, 11, 13).

Later the dove appears again in the Song of Solomon

(2:14): 'O my dove, in the clefts of the rock, in the covert of the cliff, let me see your face, let me hear your voice, for your voice is sweet, and your face is comely.' Here she appears as the intimate symbol of the World-Soul, uniting with the awakening human 'I' as comprehension through knowledge.

In the Psalms (55:6; 68:13) it is said: 'O, that I had wings like a dove! I would fly away, and be at rest.' Or 'Though they stay among the sheepfolds [they gleam like] the wings of a dove covered with silver, its pinions with green gold.' Here is the lifting up of the soul, which leads out of the trouble and distress of this world.

In the prophets the dove appears once more. We read in Isaiah: 'Like a swallow or a crane I clamour, I moan like a dove. My eyes are weary with looking upward. O Lord, I am oppressed; be thou my security!' (38:14). And Jeremiah says: 'Leave the cities, and dwell in the rock, O inhabitants of Moab! Be like the dove that nests in the sides of the mouth of a gorge' (48:28). Here the dove appears as a fugitive, returning from the towns to the rocks of the coasts, from which it had once come to the human settlements.

In the religions of the Near East the dove was held sacred. The Goddess Ishtar in Babylon was specially connected with it, and doves were sacrificed to her. Doves were consecrated in the same way to Astarte. They drew the chariot of Aphrodite; Venus Anadyomene was hatched from an egg by a dove. At the sanctuary of Zeus at Dodona, in northern Greece, doves lived in the sacred oaks and gave the answer, as holy oracles to the questions of the faithful. In the Phoenician language the same word was used for dove and for priest; in Hebrew the word for dove is the same as the Arabic word for priest. When Herodotus says that Phoenicians once brought a priestess from Thebes to Dodona, it could be either a priestess or a dove that is meant; the words are identical. It is known too that in the festivals of Adonis doves were burned in honour of the god; and Aeneas was led by doves to the Golden Bough.

From all these indications it can be seen that doves accompanied men in their migrations, that they were held sacred in connection with sacrificial ritual, and that they were attached not only to human habitations but also to temples and places of the mysteries.

2 Habitat of doves and pigeons

All domestic pigeons are descended from one species, the rock-dove, *Columba livia*. This species is distinguished by its way of life. Wild pigeons in general belong to the woods, living in trees; they are to be found all over the earth where there are woods or regions rich in trees. Neither in the far north, in tundra or steppe, nor in mountains beyond the tree limit are there pigeons. Everywhere else they are at home. More than five hundred species are known.

Only the rock-dove does not need woods. It lives on cliffs and rocks, and in ruined buildings, as the prophet says. It is found in Europe on some northern islands. It is especially numerous in County Donegal in Ireland, and lives all along the West Coast of Scotland, the Hebrides, the Orkneys and Shetlands, the Faeroes and the small rocky island of Rennesöy near Stavanger in Norway. It dwells in rocks and cliffs round the Mediterranean; in Greece, Spain and Italy, France and North Africa. It is at home in the Levant and Syria, and lives all over Asia Minor and Persia, reaching as far as the Himalayan region. If one considers the distribution of the rock-dove, it looks as if this bird occupies the great paths of human migration. From India through Persia to Asia Minor, and then along the Mediterranean coasts, everywhere rock-doves are to be found. Through thousands of years the post-Atlantean civilizations moved in this way from east to west. The rock-doves found in these regions, however, are often domestic pigeons which withdrew from human settlements and returned to a free life. Brehm writes (1911):

> In Egypt I saw them on cliffs, particularly near rapids. In India they are among the commonest birds, laying their eggs in holes and on ledges in rocks and cliffs, if possible near water. Here, as in Egypt, they are in a half-wild condition and occupy old, quiet buildings, city walls, pagodas, rock temples and such edifices.

From this description it can be seen that between the rock-dove and the domestic pigeon there is a gradual transition, and that the domestic birds can easily pass over into their wild or semi-wild condition. Certainly the main division among pigeons is not between those that are wild and those that are domesticated, but between those which live in woods, and those which have their homes in rocks and in human settlements.

Rudolf Steiner often indicated that the peoples who migrated eastwards after the decline of Atlantis crossed Europe and Asia by two great routes. Through this there later developed two distinct, widespread peoples; the Iranians to the south, the Turanians more to the north (1965, 30f [1910 Sep 1]):

> Thus there arose what is perhaps one of the greatest antitheses in the whole of post-Atlantean evolution: the antithesis between these more northerly peoples and the Iranians. Among the Iranians the longing arose to take a hand in what was going on around them, to live settled lives, to acquire possessions through effort, in other words, to apply man's spiritual forces in order to achieve the transformation of Nature. That was the strongest urge in the Iranians. And in the immediately adjacent lands to the North, lived the people who saw into the spiritual world, were on familiar terms, so to speak, with the spiritual beings, but were

wanderers, having no inclination for work and without any interest in furthering culture in the physical world.

Here there is a similar polarity to that described among the pigeons. The wild wood-pigeons are like the Turanians, and the rock-doves, which can become domestic pigeons, are like the Iranians. If we think of Noah's action in sending out the three doves at the end of the Flood, we see in a picture the beginning of the migrations to the east; the differentiation into the northern and southern groups is present also in the separation of the two main groups of pigeons. It can indeed be assumed that the wood-pigeons accompanied the Turanians, the rock-doves the Iranians, on their journey from west to east. Thus the rock-dove was tamed and domesticated, and made its home both in the sacred and the profane parts of the Iranian settlements when these became established. Doves have thus a close link with human existence.

3 Feeding and flight

The fact that the Iranians became settled led to the emergence, in the domestic pigeons which came to live with them, of a peculiar characteristic; the capacity to find their home abode again from hundreds of miles away. Many other birds have this capacity, but only when they are carrying out their long annual migrations. The pigeon can do it, with a little training, at any time of year. Thus carrier pigeons were used from antiquity; they were already known in Egypt. When Rameses III came to the throne, the news was sent all over Egypt by carrier pigeon. Besieged cities used carrier pigeons to communicate with the rest of the world, a method rendered out of date only by wireless telegraphy at the beginning of this century. As recently as the siege of Paris in the war of 1870–1, many reports were brought to and from Paris by carrier pigeon.

This transmission of messages through a kind of homing instinct, which is so deeply rooted among pigeons that they can find the way back over great distances, even at night and through regions entirely unknown to them, is a very remarkable characteristic. The peacefulness, gentleness, and the family sense of pigeons so often noticed, are related to this. It is hard to say, as the observations are not definite enough, whether it is really true that a pair of pigeons remains together inseparably over the years.

But one thing is certain; among all the birds, the various kinds of pigeon have a characteristic belonging to them alone. They feed their young with a milky juice, prepared within their own body, like most of the mammals, and man in particular, which feed their new-born with their own substance, milk, to begin with. Among the pigeons it is not only the mother which forms this substance, but both parents. No other bird has this characteristic. Many indeed have the organ, the so-called crop, in which dove-milk is developed — but only pigeons produce it. The crop is an often considerable widening of the alimentary canal, at about the point where the neck meets the breast. In other birds, and pigeons as well, it is used to mix food with saliva, and to begin the digestive process.

With pigeons, however, in the middle of the brood period the crop begins to swell, and to increase in size. Gradually the inner layers of the mucous membrane of the crop become so fat, that they desquamate, and the mass of cells is gradually dissolved in the cavity of the crop and becomes a kind of white broth, which is given to the young brood as food. This 'milk' is rich in fats and proteins, and for about three weeks it is the only food of the young pigeons; only after that can they begin to take grain.

It could easily be said that it is not a real milk, but only something popularly described as such. But there is a very significant fact on the other side. The milk of mammals and of man, which is formed in the mammary glands, is connected with a hormone produced in the pituitary gland. This hormone, called prolactin, stimulates milk production considerably; the supply of prolactin equips the milk glands for the production of milk. But the same substance can stimulate the pigeon's crop to form dove-milk and this happens so regularly that this method is a quantitative test for prolactin.

Thus there can be no doubt that dove-milk is related to mammalian milk not only by its name, but belongs to the same group of substances and is a real 'milk'. It can be assumed that the close family relationship among the pigeons, their readiness to settle and their peacefulness are connected with this formation of milk. For the young pigeon receives a food-stuff peculiar to its kind, which attaches it much more strongly to the protection of the nest and to the family than is ever the case with other birds. A part of the bodily substance of the parents is given to the young brood over many weeks, and the blood-relationship with the whole species is thus deeply influenced. The milk is a living bond holding together through the generations doves as a species in the most intimate way. Thus the rock-dove can change so easily into the domestic pigeon, and back again.

4 The crop and the larynx

In antiquity doves were called 'the guests of the gods'. They chose as their abodes temple buildings above all, and settled in the holy precincts of the mysteries. Wherever in Asia, in Europe and in North Africa temples stood, they were continually encircled by the flight of doves. The rock-dove with its brilliant grey-blue and green feathers became gradually the white temple-dove, which was used as a sacrificial animal in the most varied civilizations. In the New Testament too we find references to this. Thus doves became not only the companions of men, but were drawn into the holiest rites that men can perform. In the groves of mysteries the doves settle, and make their homes around the holy buildings.

They were messengers, and brought over great distances what human beings wished to communicate; this was only expected of them, because they were felt not only as guests but also as messengers of the gods. And as they brought tidings from the gods to men, men used them as messengers among themselves as well.

Rudolf Steiner described the task of birds in general in the cosmos, showing that it is their vocation to spiritualize matter (1970, 85 [1923 Oct 27]):

> One can actually say that, when the earth has reached the end of its existence, this earth-matter will have been spiritualized, and that the bird-creation had its place in the whole economy of earthly existence for the purpose of carrying back this spiritualized earth-matter into spirit-land.

If this is the work of the birds in general, then a particular species must surely have the task of transforming special kinds of earthly substance back into the spiritual. Could it not be that the doves have a particular duty? They give to men's settlements their company, and are thus concerned with buildings and houses. They are connected with substances used by humans. For wood, stone, mortar and everything else used in building is altered by the work spent upon it. And all these buildings are permeated by the human *word*. In and around the houses and temples, the grave-monuments and the palaces, human speech is used, and unites with the walls. And the doves become the messengers who release the human word, in its endless variety, from its enclosure in matter, and embody it again in the spiritual substance of the cosmos.

All that men have spoken, all the good and the bad that is clothed in words, is reunited with the cosmos through the function of the doves. Their work as messengers is only an earthly picture for their cosmic task. They are bearers of the Word, and they are prepared for this in their infancy. The milk given by father and mother holds them to the work that is to be done. For the bird's crop is situated anatomically where in man there is the larynx. In the larynx the word is produced, but in the pigeon's crop milk.

Mammalian milk has a definite task; it enables the new-born child to form bone substance in the right way. For milk is not just a general means of nutrition; it is specially prepared to form the material for the skeleton. Through receiving milk the human child becomes a citizen of earth; the mineral scaffolding of his bones is hardened by milk, and becomes the rock sustaining his existence.

The milk produced by doves has the task of anchoring their mission in the realm of the human word. The skeleton is intimately connected with speech; only the human race, with a skeleton which has become the image of the whole universe, can speak. Man's head is round like the universe above him; his ribs follow in their form the paths of sun and planets; his limbs are like pillars, permeated with the forces of the earth. This perfection of shape makes possible a larynx which can become the cradle of the sounding Word.

Human milk, arising in the mammary glands, provides the material substance from which the bones, an image of the whole universe, can be shaped. It is a material which conforms to the cosmic forces, and serves them. This enables the sounding Word to speak in man.

Dove's milk, arising in the realm of the larynx occupied by the bird's crop, helps towards the redemption of the spoken Word, which has united with the matter shaped by human hands. From the grave of matter the dove liberates the human Word.

Man and dove become companions who have journeyed together into the land of earth, to become servants of the Word. Therefore doves are 'the guests of the gods'.

For this reason the words for 'dove' and 'priest' are almost identical in many languages. For this reason Noah sent the dove out of the ark, to find out whether the earth had become as hard as bone again, so that it could be trodden by human feet. For this reason the dove is 'the darling of her mother, flawless to her that bore her' as the Song of Solomon declares (6:9).

5 The dove and the Word

The dove appears too above the head of Jesus of Nazareth, when John baptizes him in the Jordan. Rudolf Steiner says about this (1982, 184f [1909 July 3]):

> While in a physical incarnation something spiritual descends from higher worlds and unites with the physical, that which was sacrificed in order that the Christ Spirit might enter appeared above the head of Jesus of Nazareth in the form of a white dove. Something spiritual appears as it detaches itself from the physical. That is an actual clairvoyant observation and it would be far from right to consider it a mere allegory or symbol. It is a real, clairvoyant, spiritual fact, actually present on the astral plane to clairvoyant sight. Just as a physical birth implies the attraction of spirit, so this birth was a sacrifice, a renunciation; and thereby the opportunity was provided for the Spirit, Who at the beginning of our *Earth* evolution *moved upon the face of the waters*, to unite with the threefold sheath of Jesus of Nazareth and to strengthen and inspire it through and through, as described.

The dove appears here as the result of the sacrifice through which the Logos, the Spirit, who brooded over the waters (Gen.1:2) could draw into a human body. Thus here too the dove becomes a helper of the 'Word'. The Logos permeates the body right down into the bony system, into the earthly substance which is prepared by milk. At this holy place of human history, at the Baptism in Jordan, the true being of the group-soul of the doves is revealed. Through its sacrifice the place is prepared which is to be filled by the cosmic Word itself. Until then it has been guest and messenger of the gods; now it gives up this task, for the Logos itself has assumed it. Perhaps once, when men built the Tower of Babel, and their original language suffered the fate of fragmentation, the doves began to prepare to lead the divided, splintered human word back to the realm from which it once came. But then the Logos itself entered the earthly world, and the task of the doves was thereby completed for the time; their priestly duty carried out, their mission fulfilled.

Today they have become commonplace. The mystery temples are ruined, and so pigeons live in squares and market-places, a picture of how the word is wasted and misused. As in the past, they pick up words, keep them and bring them back into the spiritual world. They have become messengers of men. In German they are called *Taube*. Etymology does not connect this, as might seem likely with *taub*, deaf, dull, 'dumb', but regards it as imitative, representing the coo of doves.* However this may be, the pigeon today seems a stupid creature, because its true being and character cannot be recognized.

In the future its light will shine again, and reveal its glory where sacrifice and ministering messenger-service count for more than powerful appearance. The saying: 'I was naked, and you clothed me' applies to the doves. They gave back their function, their work in the service of the Word, to him who as Logos came unto his own.

---

*Eric Partridge, *Origins*, says that 'dove' and 'deaf' are perhaps connected.

The Sparrows of the Earth

1 The life of the sparrow

Wherever people live and have settled the sparrow is at home. In the many and various names used for him in Germany* we can hear the sympathy but also the slight disrespect with which people regard him. Few are really friendly towards him. One puts up with him as a habit; who bothers about sparrows? They are so numerous and commonplace that they are hardly noticed. And yet they are our companions and settle wherever humans are established.

There is hardly a farmhouse, village, market-place or suburban street which has no sparrows. And the more densely people live together, the more noisily do the sparrow hordes bustle about. In the midst of big cities, on main roads, in backyards and gardens and in the smaller parks they are at home. Where people crowd together, where children play, vehicles clatter and lovers embrace, where life and death daily touch hands — there also the sparrows twitter.

Grey, almost like ashes, is the feather garment of the house-sparrow. Around the eye and beak it is somewhat darker, with a brownish stripe running from the back of the eyes — at both sides of the head — towards the neck. The wings are brown and dark on top, blackish brown on the underside. No yellow or red, no blue — only a few white patches adorn the little bird. He is really insignificant and without special markings.

*Hausspatz, Haussperling, Hofspatz, Rauchspatz, Dieb, Sperk, Hausfink, Mistfink.

But when you know him more intimately and make friends with his appearance, his habits and peculiarities, his deeds and doings, then he becomes lovable and quite remarkably friendly and interesting, for he knows life and fits himself as modestly into it as circumstances allow. He possesses his nest for himself alone; no-one may cross his path there. But he does not object if another sparrow builds a nest near him and moves into it. Husband and wife — if they live long enough — often remain true to each other for years for they stay by the nest they have set up or found for themselves. The nest is home, security and possession.

As much as they are preoccupied with their own nests, just as much do they like going about in the company of other sparrows. One will seldom find a single sparrow. Wherever they loiter around, they appear by the dozen. They are so similar that it is difficult to distinguish them from one another. Their games, movements and reactions are almost identical. They like to quarrel, chatter with one another, hop, tumble about in the sand and puddles of the street, whirr over the pavement and suddenly fly off, back to the nest, soon returning to rejoin their brothers and sisters.

Just as ordinary as their colours are, just as simple and limited is the rest of their bird-existence. They can chirp and twitter a little, but it is not given to them to sing. House-sparrows also make no great excursions. In autumn they stay in their nests; the unrest and fever of migration is alien to them. At the beginning of August, or somewhat later, they go away, always together with their wives, for a little holiday into the nearby country-side, mostly near ripening cornfields. They rent a summer residence in the hedges surrounding the fields and there they play and peck, bathe and sleep. On some days the pair go back to the nest to see if everything at home is still in order; but soon they appear again in the fields.

If these summer guests are very numerous, the farmer

will have difficulty in bringing in a full harvest for sparrows can eat without stopping. But if there is not much grain, all kinds of beetles, grasshoppers, caterpillars and worms are also consumed. But only the quite young sparrows like such animal food; the adults prefer corn and other seeds.

When autumn comes they all fly back to town. The waiting nest is newly upholstered and lined and prepared for the winter. Seldom do coupling and egg-laying come about at this time. Only in really warm autumn weeks is there still some springtime romance. It is more like a second summer, mostly without visible results.

Sparrows can have quite long lives if nothing cuts them short. Their average life-span is seven to eight years. Some reach their eleventh or twelfth year before they die. But the nests last longer. If one member of a pair dies, the nest will provide for a male or female joining the survivor. And so it goes on, a kind of life-quadrille, with the nest always as its centre.*

2 Nesting and habitat

In Bachelard (1960) we read:

When we observe a nest we find ourselves at the source of a trust towards the world, we touch on a focal point of trust, we are struck by an appeal to cosmic trust. Would a bird build his nest if he did not have an instinctive trust in the world? . . . In order to experience this trust . . . we do not need to count up the material reasons for it.

For they hardly exist. What is at hand is based — with people as well as with a bird — on this 'cosmic trust', which ever anew goes about setting up a nest, a house, a dwelling, a home of one's own, where protection is sought and also found.

*These descriptions and others in this study are based on D. Summers-Smith 1963.

The place of security, the feeling of being protected, is one of the original needs of man on earth. Many birds also share in this. But it is not a drive which — as many psychologists believe — makes us want to return to the warm seclusion of the womb which protected us before birth. That would not be trust but anxiety. We would not go back into the original condition of our existence but forwards into the future of our destiny on earth.

A bird seeks no refuge. He builds his nest in trust towards his future generations which will carry further what he passes on to them.

A bird's nest can hardly be compared with the dens and holes, the shelters and lairs of other animals, for a bird *builds* his nest: he forms it and equips it. He uses feathers and branches, grass and twigs, stones and clay, straw and mortar. There are birds which weave their nests and others which make them firm with saliva, which turns into a kind of mortar on drying. In trees and bushes, in clay and sand, in grass and on rocks, birds' nests are built. A bird first touches upon earth-existence in the nest. For him it is the support, the foundation, on which his existence rests. Without a nest he would have soared away into the widths of the air. But his house keeps him fixed to the earth; it is a placenta through which he remains living within the earth-circumference. But the ability to build a nest is at the same time the umbilical cord which binds him to it.

For other creatures the nest is a refuge and a shelter. With few exceptions (some fish, the beaver, for example) the nest is not built but searched for and found, or it can be dug and scooped out.

The sparrows give their name to by far the largest order of the bird world. They are the Passerines, with about five thousand different species.

The Passerines are spread over the whole earth and inhabit woods, heaths, moor, tundra, high mountains, steppes, deserts, reedy thickets and

open, tree-covered country . . . They are originally
tree or shrub dwellers, as most of them still are
today, yet there are some species, such as the larks
and fallow-finches, which have adapted themselves
completely to life on the ground. Some kinds . . .
are almost incapable of flight. (Makatsch 1954).
And Brehm (1913) said of them:

They are children of the land. As far as plant-growth
reaches, their living area extends. In woods they are
more abundant than in areas without woods . . .
Many kinds live almost exclusively on the ground
and most of them are not at all unaccustomed to it.
Very few shun the vicinity of people; many invite
themselves as guests to the master of the earth in so
far as they trustfully visit his house and farm
premises, his orchard and flower garden.

Crows and jackdaws and magpies, finches and bullfinches,
larks and tits, thrushes, wrens, nightingales, swallows and
hedge-sparrows are members of this order. All are birds
which are connected with human beings.

But among them — perhaps bound most deeply to the
earth and to people — the house-sparrow forms a special
breed, for no other bird comes so close to man. One
could almost say that he alienates himself from nature —
in the manner of domestic animals — in order to become
part of the human kingdom. But the sparrow does not
forsake his own form, as do all the varied types of dog.
Nor does he lose himself in a special activity as do hens
and cows in producing eggs and milk. The sparrow is not
a domestic creature yet he lives as close to man as few
other creatures do.

The architects' guild ought to carry the sparrow on
their coats of arms. Streets and squares, courtyards and
gardens have become a natural environment for sparrows.
They build their nests where people live. Under the roof
ridge, behind the gutter, in the shelter of the chimney,
at the edge of dormer windows. But the nests are also

set up in the branches of trees and bushes where these are close to people's houses.

When sparrows were introduced into America in the middle of the last century it was observed that they appeared in larger, then in smaller towns, after that in villages and hamlets, finally on single farms. But if they are brought to a farm near a township, in a district where there are not too many of them, they will leave the farm and withdraw to the township. (Summers-Smith 1963, 209).

Yes, they look for the proximity of many human dwellings. There, where dust and waste, rubbish and refuse accumulate, out of straw and paper, hay and wool, hair and threads, twigs and grass-stalks, the sparrow builds his nest. It is not a very skilfully made house; from the outside it often looks dishevelled and without plan. But inside it is smooth, well-lined and warm. A roof always arches over it so that it becomes a real hut. Only when tree hollows or breeding cages are at hand is the vaulted roof omitted.

The material for nest building is brought together from everywhere. Above all the inner bark of twigs and branches is torn off for this purpose, and sparrows have even been seen daring to approach doves in order to pluck out feathers for their nests. No wonder that one of their many names is 'thief' or 'robber'.

The nest, once built, is lived in and guarded at all seasons apart from the 'holiday' weeks. No other sparrow may approach it; females drive off females, and males the males. Hardly ever does one sex dare to challenge the other. That is a strictly maintained taboo.

Mating, egg laying and rearing take place in spring and summer. Around Easter the female lays an egg every morning for about a week. From two to eight eggs are laid, depending on the age of the parents and on whether the season is early or late. The average brooding time is twelve days, but longer and shorter periods have been observed. As with all Passerines, new-born sparrows are naked and helpless. They have to be fed and warmed by the parents. But in less than three weeks they have grown up into little sparrows; they leave the nest and begin to look after themselves. Their parents then bother no more about them, even refusing them access to the old nest, for by this time a new brood is on the way.

Each sparrow pair breeds at least twice a year; some manage three or four broods, so the rapid increase of sparrow population is not surprising. As long as the brood is still young the parents care for it with touching devotion. They ward off, to the point of self-sacrifice, any attack on the little ones. Many observations have established this.

But as soon as the young have learned to fly, it is the turn of the next generation to take up their whole attention. So between ten and twenty young ones are hatched out and brought up by one set of parents quite soon after their first mating. Only when the third or even fourth brood has grown up, after midsummer, do the parents go away into the countryside. They have accomplished their work and can now devote themselves to the joys of existence. Other parents appear and young sparrows begin to spread out among the older ones and to claim their own living-space. Soon they will set up nests for the winter and will find mates. In the following spring they will begin to breed.

How quickly all that goes! Nevertheless everything is ordered and ordained. It is said in the Gospel: 'Are not two sparrows sold for a penny? And not one of them will fall to the ground without your Father's will' (Matt. 10:29).

3 Sparrows and man

During the last hundred years sparrows have started an astonishing conquest across the earth. In the middle of the last century they were unknown in North America. Towards the end of the sixties they were brought to various East Coast cities, and in a few decades they spread across almost the whole continent. By the end of the century they had penetrated as far as San Francisco. In 1889 W.B. Barrow wrote (quoted in Summers-Smith 1963, 176): 'From this time (1875) to the present, the marvellous rapidity of the sparrow's multiplication, the surpassing swiftness of its extension, and the prodigious size of the area it has overspread are without parallel in the history of any bird.' It was a triumphal procession of the sparrow from the east to the west of North America.

At the turn of the century South America — especially Argentina, Chile, Peru and Bolivia — was conquered in a similar way. In Australia and New Zealand the coastal districts were populated at the same time by all kinds of sparrows. Today one can truly say that all continents and — with few exceptions — all countries and regions are densely colonized by house-sparrows and allied species.

Their adaptability is astonishing. They are not bound to definite climatic and environmental conditions, as are many other birds. They can maintain themselves in subarctic districts just as well as in tropical regions and deserts. They are as much at home in Kiruna in northern Sweden as in Cuiabá in central Brazil. They live and nest also in barren Aden and tropical Burma.

There is obviously an intimate connection between sparrows and human settlements. In America one could observe that they pushed forward with the construction crews along new railway lines that were being built, from one inhabited place to the next. They always favoured settlements which had streets and squares, not isolated houses.

When empty houses stand free for nest-building, they avoid this opportunity, for the house sparrow 'will normally only nest in unoccupied buildings, if they are close to inhabited ones.' (Summers-Smith 1963, 209).

During the Second World War sparrows moved with the British Eighth Army through the North African desert and settled in their camping places. In 1956 a whole colony of sparrows had settled deep under the earth in a coal-mine in Northumberland, England, and were being fed by the miners. But this intimate connection between men and sparrows is optional, since we find sparrows also living, for example, on the uninhabited islands around New Zealand and in the deserted plateaus of North India.

In spite of these exceptions — or perhaps just because of them — the connection of these birds with the human race is so astonishing as to be of a quite special kind. What is it that links the sparrow to man? Is it man himself, or something else connected with him?

Sparrows always remain shy and wary towards people. Very seldom do they become tame and trusting, and attempts to get them to breed in captivity have not worked well. They lay only a few eggs and go about the business of bringing up their young in a dispirited way. They remain always on their guard when a human being approaches them.

They can indeed be cheeky and will intrude boldly into kitchens and living-rooms to fetch food that appeals to them. But they stay for seconds only and fly off as quickly as they came. They live near, but by no means *with* us.

It is rather as if they like to dwell in the shadow of our human activities. Where we have worked and built, where traffic rolls and machines operate — in railway halls and factory buildings, in streets and houses — there sparrows like to live. There, in the refuse of our activity, in dust and soot and smoke and sand, the sparrows find a world which suits them.

This cannot have been always so. For only in the last

hundred years has this progressive industrialization of human existence taken place. Where were the sparrows earlier? Their history and gradual development is unclear. Some believe that they have pushed forward step by step from Asia to Europe; others believe that their origin is to be traced in Africa, whence they advanced north along the Nile valley. The various kinds of sparrows (rock sparrows, Italian and Spanish sparrows) which intermingled in many parts of the earth, have concealed their previous history.

But one thing is clearly to be seen: the gradual spreading of sparrows occurred in earlier millennia along the paths of farming peoples. Wherever people settled down to till the land, the sparrows who had come with them settled too. They became the farmer's companion, without ever coming close to him.

Perhaps we may outline the following history of the sparrows on earth: first they went with the farmers and the bounty of the harvest. Then they accompanied man into his larger settlements and towns; and finally — from the last century on — they have gone with him into the industrial world he has built up around himself.

The report from a Northumberland coal mine indicates a further step. Accompanying man, the house-sparrows dip into the depths of earth-substance. Yet they remain an independent race which has not lost its gay artlessness, its liking for play and pleasure, its spontaneous chatter and its trust in the world. They carry their bird life into the depths of the earth and yet retain their own nature.

4 A Christmas story

Once the sparrows were like other wild birds. They built their nests in trees and bushes, lived in the open world of meadows and steppes, on mountains and in the plains where brooks and rivers flow. At that time they could still sing and — like larks and finches, tits and starlings

— make their voices resound into the widths of space. In those long ago days they still went on great journeys, moving south in autumn and back to the north in spring.

Today young sparrows get their food mainly from insects and only a little from grain. The older sparrows have given up meat and prefer grain. This indicates that a gradual transformation of feeding habits has taken place. In the days when sparrows were still a proud, free race, they ate what nature offered them: spiders and beetles, grasshoppers and caterpillars and many other little creatures.

But step by step, they have given up the freedom of the wild. Their singing changed into chirping, twittering and chattering. The great migrations were discontinued, for man had begun to settle on the earth. He broke up the ground with his plough and sowed the seeds of the grasses that were to be transformed into grain for bread. Then the various wild sparrows came, looked at this human activity and found it right and good.

They reported what they had seen to their guiding spirit, who carried it further into the heights, and the angels found out what was happening on earth. The news rose to yet higher spheres: 'Man is cultivating the earthly ground,' it sounded. 'He sows and harvests and prepares his bread.' It was a beautiful song that sounded through heaven.

Now to the guiding spirit of sparrows came back the call that their creatures should accompany man at his work. 'Put aside your colourful clothing; forego your song; go to live near the children of men. Let your food be the corn; your nests the roofs of human habitations.'

The sparrows on earth heard this call and their hearts began to beat faster. 'O what misery,' they twittered. 'O what joy,' chirped others. 'Yes, we will bear it and do it.'

Since then the sparrow's heart beats ten times more quickly than that of man; 800 times a minute, 48 000 times an hour and over a million times a day. Their breathing also is rapid; 200 breaths a minute, when they hop or fly, or when it is very hot outside. And their body warmth is much higher than feverous temperature in humans. These little birds are unpretentious but warm, with their hearts beating so fast that we can no longer distinguish the single beats and normally cannot count them. For us they are like a light, anxious fluttering.

But for the sparrows it is joy for they are responding to their guiding spirits, who had heard the message of the heavenly choirs. But hidden in those words was a mysterious proclamation which neither sparrow nor sparrow-spirit could decipher. It sounded something like this: 'When people grind flour out of corn, when they bake bread out of flour and water, leaven and salt, and take it as nourishment, when the earth is transformed under the burden of the growing ears — then a Child shall be born who will carry the Light. To him should your bird creatures be of service.'

Although the divine message was not understood it was none the less heard, carried to earth and imprinted in the hearts, beaks and wings of the sparrow tribes. Now the sparrows go where human beings go — into the darkness of earth and the realms of decayed matter; into the dust and the shadows.

But with them goes a delicate ray of light, fine as a breath, which only children on Christmas Eve can sometimes see. For the sparrows have become poor; their garment is grey, like poverty, and brown like the homely bread of earth. But in this garment of contentment lives the cheerfulness of small joys and the blessing of trust.

'What harm can the darkness do us?' beats the sparrow heart. 'The message is fulfilled, the Child is born, and light breaks into the darkness of earth. Down to the dust and the refuse, down to the depths of the earth, it penetrates, and we' — so the sparrow tongues twitter — 'perceive its shining.'

A CHRISTMAS STORY

Messengers of Christmas are the sparrows. They accompany man and yet remain strangers to him. But one day, when in his heart also the light of Christmas begins to shine, they will become tame. Then they will sit on his shoulders and pick breadcrumbs from his hands. And some will hold these crumbs in their beaks and will place the crumbs of joy on the lips of the children of men. That will be a joyous message for many angels in heaven.

Bibliography

Bachelard, Gaston. 1960. *Poetik des Raumes*. München.

Brehm, Alfred. 1911. *Vögel*. Vol. 1. (Vol. 6 of *Tierleben*). Leipzig: Bibliogr. Institut.

——1913. *Vögel*. Vol. 4. (Vol. 9 of *Tierleben*). Leipzig: Bibliogr. Institut.

Gerlach, Richard. 1953. *Die Gefiederten*. Hamburg.

Makatsch, Wolfgang. 1954. *Die Vögel der Erde*. Berlin.

Oken, Lorenz. 1837. *Allgemeine Naturgeschichte für alle Stände*. Stuttgart.

Partridge, Eric. 1966. *Origins. Ashort Elymological Dictioinary*.

Siewert, Horst. 1955. *Störche*. Gütersloh.

Steiner, Rudolf. 1905 December 3. Unpublished lecture held at Köln.

——1947 [1922]. *The Mystery of the Trinity*. London: Steiner, & New York: Anthroposophic.

——1963 [1911]. *Wonders of the World, Trials of the Soul, Revelations of the Spirit*. London: Steiner.

——1965 [1910]. *The Gospel of St Matthew*. London: Steiner.

——1970 [1923]. *Man as Symphony of the Creative Word*. London: Steiner.

——1982 [1909]. *The Gospel of St John and its Relation to the Other Gospels*. New York: Anthroposophic.

Summers-Smith, D. 1963. *The House Sparrow*. London: Collins.

Penguins
Seals, Dolphins, Salmon and Eels

Karl König

The first part of König's sketches for an imaginative zoology.

Published 1984

Elephants
Bears, horses, cats and dogs

Karl König

The final part of König's sketches for an imaginative zoology.

Publication 1988

Floris Books

The Human Soul

Karl König

The attributes of the soul's landscape are described: pain, anxiety, fear, shame, and anger, concluding with a chapter on dreams.

The First Three Years of The Child

Karl König

The author examines the first three years of the life of the child in the light of the three major achievements that dominate them: learning to walk, speak and think.

Brothers and Sisters

The order of birth in the family
Karl König

The fact of being a first, second or third child determines how we approach life and its demands.

Floris Books
Anthroposophic Press

Scientist of the Invisible

An introduction of the life and work of Rudolf Steiner

A P Shepherd
Foreword by Owen Barfield

Written to counter widespread lack of knowledge about Steiner, the first part of the book is biographical and the second part penetrates deeply into his work.

Rudolf Steiner Enters My Life

Friedrich Rittelmeyer

Rittelmeyer writes of his many conversations with one of the most important figures of our time. He chronicles his ten years of apprehension, critical investigation and cautious scrutiny of the new body of thought.

Floris Books